TIME-OUT
FOR PARENTS
REVISED EDITION

A GUIDE TO
COMPASSIONATE PARENTING

CHERI HUBER
MELINDA GUYOL, MFT

Books by Cheri Huber

From Keep It Simple Books
The Key and the Name of the Key Is Willingness
How You Do Anything Is How You Do Everything: A Workbook
There Is Nothing Wrong With You: Going Beyond Self-Hate
The Depression Book: Depression as an Opportunity for Spiritual Growth
The Fear Book: Facing Fear Once and for All
Nothing Happens Next: Responses to Questions about Meditation
Be the Person You Want to Find: Relationship and Self-Discovery
Sex and Money...are dirty, aren't they? A Guided Journal
Suffering Is Optional: Three Keys to Freedom and Joy
When You're Falling, Dive: Acceptance, Possibility and Freedom
Time-Out for Parents: A Guide to Compassionate Parenting
The Monastery Cookbook: Stories and Recipes from A Zen Kitchen

From A Center for the Practice of Zen Buddhist Meditation
That Which You Are Seeking Is Causing You to Seek

From Hay House
How to Get from Where You Are to Where You Want to Be

From Present Perfect Books (Sara Jenkins, editor)
Trying to Be Human: Zen Talks from Cheri Huber
Turning Toward Happiness: Conversations with a Zen Teacher and Her Students
Good Life: A Zen Precepts Retreat with Cheri Huber
Buddha Facing the Wall: Interviews with American Zen Monks
Sweet Zen: Dharma Talks with Cheri Huber

Videotapes from Openings
There Are No Secrets: Zen Meditation with Cheri Huber
Yoga for Meditators *with Christa Rypins*
Yoga for A Better Back *with Christa Rypins and Dr. John Sousa*
Yummy Yoga: Stress Relief for Hips, Back, and Neck *with Christa Rypins*

Audiotape from Who's Here? Productions
Getting Started Going Deeper: Introduction to Meditation

All books are available through your local bookstore.

Acknowledgments

I, Cheri, would like to thank Monique and Brian for their patience and understanding as I continue to learn compassionate parenting.

Melinda and I would like to thank the following people for their ideas, experiences and willingness:
Jan Rogerson, Darlene Baumgartner, Jan Leimert, Jan Letendre, Christine Taylor, Cameron Sellar.

Thank you once again to June Shiver who has employed her creative talents to produce a book we hope most people will find friendly, approachable, and fun to read.

Introduction

As Zen meditation teachers, we teach people to sit in silence, facing a blank wall. The idea is to learn to slow down, to become quiet in mind and body, subtle in attention. This practice can enable us to experience who we really are, our True Nature, our essence, God. Variations of this practice are found in all major religions throughout history.

In the system of controlling children's behavior called "time-out," angry or misbehaving children are isolated, made to be quiet, and sometimes even required to sit facing a wall. This method has been in vogue long enough that we are now receiving students who, when asked to sit quietly by themselves in meditation, feel punished, feel "bad."

Our experience is that much of the discussion and literature on parenting focuses on the parent-child interaction, specifically on how to get the child to behave. It seems to us that a vital aspect of the interaction is then neglected. That aspect is the parent's internal process.

This book is about changing the concept of time-out. Instead of punishing children by sending them into isolation, let's offer ourselves time-out to discover our own needs, and

our own true
selves. Then we
will have everything
WE need in order
to give our children
what THEY need.

... but wait!
What's going on
with me?

You cannot give to your child
until you can give to yourself!

Our hope is that this book will demon-
strate how that is so and encourage a
more compassionate way of parenting
our children and ourselves.

In loving kindness,
Cheri and Melinda

For all the children
who are,
who were,
who will be

Table of Contents

TIME-OUT FOR PARENTS
REVISED EDITION

A GUIDE TO COMPASSIONATE PARENTING

JAN AND ALIX*

I had come to dread picking up my
five year old daughter Alix each day.
I was tense and
drained from
work pressures
and the long
commute, and
what greeted me every evening at
the daycare center was a cranky,
whiney, tired, hungry child. It often
seemed that her one purpose in life
was to make me more miserable.

I tried saying to Alix the kinds of
things I'd heard parents say.

*You will meet Jan and Alix several times throughout
the book.

"Stop whining and crying."

" We'll be home in five minutes
so stop it now!"

"You're giving me a headache."

Nothing I said improved the situation.
The real message I was giving Alix
was that her feelings were not okay.

I so dreaded my daughter's whining
and crying that I would steel myself
and tough it out, or I would threaten
her with "time-out." When my words
had no effect on her behavior, I
would feel out of control and resort
to raising my voice, which made me
feel like I had "lost it." I felt

defeated and inadequate; I felt like a bad parent. Many days I would end up with a headache, shouting at my daughter, with her shouting and crying in response.

I tried explaining to Alix what behavior was not okay, such as whining, shouting at me, and being noncompliant. However, because I was so tired and tense and miserable, I usually was shouting and whining, too! When explaining appropriate behavior didn't work, I sank to having candy waiting in the car,

which made me feel guilty and usually ruined Alix's appetite for dinner.

I desperately wanted to end our
suffering but could not see how to do
that. I kept looking for solutions
outside myself. I had no reserves left
to be calm,

       loving,

           and compassionate.

***

What We Want for Our Children

The approach to parenting we are
offering is based on the premise that

> we want our children to become
> happy, fulfilled adults
> who grow with life's challenges,
> and who feel good about their
> lives and themselves.

However, in working with meditation
students, we have become increasingly
aware that we are unintentionally
teaching children to be
> self-conscious,
> emotionally repressed beings
> who believe they are inherently bad.

The reason for the difference
between what we want
for our children
and how they actually develop
is that they learn more from
what we DO
and how we ARE
than from
what we SAY.

They learn from what we model

and

we model what we learned as children.

If my neighbor doesn't clean up his yard, I'm calling the police.

Johnny is your friend. You two shouldn't fight.

I'm so afraid something awful is going to happen.

Don't be afraid. There's nothing to be afraid of.

If we hope to give children the gift of a happy, responsible, fully alive adulthood, we must first live that way ourselves.

"Yes, but I can't take time for me. The children's needs have to come first."

To this widely held belief, we offer this observation, gleaned from countless airplane trips:

 A flight attendant's voice is heard on the pre-flight safety video, as oxygen masks are shown dropping from overhead compartments:

"For those traveling with small children, be sure to put your oxygen mask on first before assisting your child."

The message is clear. If you aren't alive, you can't keep your child alive. A parent whose needs aren't being met has few resources to offer a child. And to be alive requires that we pay attention to ourselves in a new way.

As you read this book,

at several points along the way you will be asked to

STOP

and take TIME-OUT to be present to yourself, to your breath, to your feelings, to your experience of the moment.

This is the most powerful

TIME-OUT

any of us can take.

Take a moment just to BE with yourself. Turn your attention to your breathing. Take a few slow, deep breaths and notice what it's like to be present to the thoughts, emotions, and sensations you are experiencing.

As you breathe, allow your attention to move into your body with your breath. Is your body tense? Relaxed?

Ask yourself, "What am I feeling?" Notice how you find the answer to that question. Where do you look to find your feelings?

Notice your thoughts. What are they saying? Are you aware that different parts of you say different things?

Simply be present in this moment, just noticing.

Emotions

Much of the focus of this little book is on emotion. Our emotions, our feelings, are not something to get through, get over, get past, or get away from. Feelings are who we are. We are feeling beings. Feeling is how we know we are alive, how we know we are human.

It is our experience that socializing children (basically, teaching them to look outward instead of inward to know what is so for them) results in sublimating their emotions and sending them into adulthood feeling bad and guilty whenever an emotion slips through. The overriding message they receive seems to be:

AN ADULT SHOULD BE IN CONTROL.
IT IS NOT POSSIBLE
TO BE IN CONTROL
IF YOU ARE EMOTIONAL.

CONCLUSION:
GET RID OF EMOTION BECAUSE
EMOTION THREATENS CONTROL.

14

EMOTION
THREATENS YOUR ABILITY
TO BE WHO YOU SHOULD BE!

OR, as a child learns it,
IT IS BAD TO FEEL.

When we hide feelings from children,
they learn:

When I grow up,
I'll have to hide my feelings
because that's what grownups do.

Think about some common messages from your childhood, and consider the times you might have passed them along to your children.

--Big boys/girls don't cry.
--Stop crying. There's nothing to cry about.
--Don't be afraid. There's nothing to be afraid of.
--Don't be shy.
--Stop feeling sorry for yourself.
--You can't be hungry, you just ate.
--You're just trying to get attention.

Through such messages, we are denying a child's experience. It might not be our intent, but what we are saying is, "Don't have your feelings. Have the feelings I want you to have," or "Don't be who you are. Be who I want you to be."

Often, information like this can lead a parent to feel guilty. But, please, no guilt here. This is not about guilt-- guilt misses the point altogether.

Instead of feeling guilty, notice that how you treat your child is probably how you were treated as a child.

Consider that
how you treat
your child
is probably
how you
were treated
as a child.

And it is how
you treat yourself.

When your child is having a temper tantrum and it makes you furious, you can guess that the people around you probably reacted with fury when you had a temper tantrum. In that moment of awareness you can step back, find a little humor, make it fun, make it playful.

☆ With awareness, you can change old patterns and use some skillful means of distraction and diversion. ☆

Examples
-- Have a "temper tantrum" of your own: Stamp your feet and yell something like, "I DON'T LIKE THIS. I HATE THIS." Yell whatever expresses your feelings in the moment.

-- Do Jumping Jacks and invite your child to join in. Ask the child to choose the next movement the two of you do.

Realize "temper tantrum" is a stage children pass through fairly quickly. Then, rather than deciding this is a terrible problem that has to be solved, you can take a TIME-OUT and look to yourself. See if you can discern what you learned in childhood that makes strong emotional displays a problem for you.

Finding the Compassionate Parent

One of the great difficulties in parenting happens when we find ourselves being the same emotional age as the child. (And the worst place of all is when we find we are emotionally younger than the child!)

For example, the child has made a huge mess with toys and possessions, and we find ourselves reacting with frustration and annoyance and saying something like, "Why do I always have to clean up your messes? Why don't you ever clean up after yourself?"

If we're paying attention, we realize "I am not the parent. I am a child, and I am in competition with the child I am supposed to be parenting." This is a wonderful moment to step back, take a deep breath, and say, "We have two children in this scene, and they both need to be parented." It can be very helpful to be able to find and draw upon an internal kind, loving, compassionate parent for both of those children, rather than letting one small child "parent" another small child.

Most of us can access the kind, loving, compassionate parent fairly easily when things are going well, when we check on the child who's sleeping like a little angel, or when the child has done something particularly sweet or loving or adorable. At these times we're aware that we love this child unconditionally and feel great tenderness and warmth and affection.

We lose sight of that when we leave the place of kind parent, and identify with a part of us who is tired, stressed, hungry, perhaps emotionally very young. If we stop for a moment, we can realize when that is happening to us.

The kind, loving parent
speaks a very different language
from the person
who is stressed and overwhelmed.
Everything about those two people is

different: one is relaxed, comfortable, open, loving; the other is tight, tense, worried, nervous, short-tempered. When we recognize we're being that overwhelmed, tired person, or when we realize we've slipped into a very young, petulant, punishing, blaming child part of ourselves, we can stop, take a deep breath and step back and see ourselves from a broader perspective.

From this clearer place, it can be a powerful experience to take a few long deep breaths and recall a time when the child was being particularly loving, a time when the child needed us and we were there. We can remember when we looked forward to being a parent, when we wanted to

have a child to raise and care for,
and we can feel our hearts open.

Just in that moment of stepping back and taking a breath, we can stop believing the story we are telling ourselves about how awful this is, how intolerable, how it shouldn't be this way, how I can't stand it. In those few breaths we can call forth the kind parental part of ourselves and change the nature of the interaction. We change it for the child and we change it for ourselves. We both receive the kindness and love.

Another way to find the compassionate parent in ourselves is to bring up an image of how we look when we're yelling at our child, for instance. Just stepping back and seeing how we (imagine) we look. What is that person feeling? What does that person need? By seeing ourselves as if we were someone outside of us, we can often find a more caring perspective.

We want to practice regularly evoking the compassionate parent, not just in stressful situations. If we practice with small things, finding compassion when we are stressed won't be so hard. We'll have experience doing it.

As we're taking TIME-OUT, we want to identify consciously with the loving part of ourselves, reminding ourselves that's how we want to be with our child, that's the choice we want to make. We practice going to that place so that, when we are in a stressful situation, the compassionate parent is close by.

When we are living
in conscious compassionate awareness,
we have the life we want
for ourselves,
and we are modeling it
for our children.

Simply put, we're learning to be for ourselves the parent we want to be for our child. When we are that parent, we feel taken care of, the child feels taken care of, our partner feels taken care of, everyone feels taken care of. Finding our way back to an unconditionally loving relationship with ourselves gives us access to the kind, compassionate, loving presence we want for our child.

It's simple. When we are living in conscious, compassionate awareness, we are for ourselves what we need, and we are for our children what they need. We are modeling the adulthood we want for our children, and what we hope they will model for their children.

Take a moment to remember some negative messages from your childhood. Write them down. Notice how you feel now as you recall how your feelings were negated then.

Taking the Opposite Approach

Trying to be with a child in ways opposite from how our parents were with us is not the answer. If we simply react against how our parents were, that's not a kind, loving, well-considered perspective from which to parent. If we adopt a system of taking the opposite approach to the one our parents took, sooner or later our system will break down.

Maybe your father yelled a lot, and you decide "I'm always going to speak softly to my children," which you can do as long as things are going well, but when you get stressed, you start yelling. And even if you're not yelling out loud, you're yelling inside. You might control yourself tighter and tighter as the stress builds--still speak in a calm and quiet voice--but your emotions are shrieking.

What we're encouraging here is coming back to a centered place from which you have the full range of responses available to you in any situation. Sometimes yelling might be the perfect thing. Sometimes speaking softly is the perfect thing.

Having a fixed formula of
How-I-Have-To-Be
is a recipe for failure
and a poor message to give a child.

It is possible to express any emotion fully and not upset anyone around us. We accomplish that by taking full responsibility for and ownership of our emotions.

I can be angry and yelling about how upset I am, but I am making it clear that
-- I know these are MY emotions,
-- I'm not upset with you,
-- I'm not blaming you,
-- it's not your fault.

In fact, with this approach, I can even enroll you in helping me express emotion.

RACHEL AND JASON

When Rachel discovered everything she had carefully packed in the car for a trip had been rearranged and nothing could be found, she let out a spontaneous yell and stomped her feet in frustration. She quickly looked at her four year old son, concerned her outburst might have frightened him, even though it wasn't directed at him. To her surprise, she saw he was simply watching her with interest, and that he then went on with his own activities. It seemed he knew Mom was just angry--nothing to fear, nothing to hide. Mom was just expressing her feelings.

★★★

It's not a particular emotion that is threatening or frightening to a child, it's how the parent feels about expressing the emotion that is frightening to the child.

When we as parents are all right with feeling and expressing strong emotions, children and others around us tend to be all right as well.

Human beings are feeling beings, and to be fully human is to have the experience of the full range of emotions: happiness, sadness, grief, rage, joy, awe. . .

Emotions, when we take the time to explore and experience them, are in our internal landscapes as the weather is in the world around us, ranging from dark and stormy to calm and sunny.

Constantly changing.
Rarely the same for very long.

Most of us were raised to believe there are "good" feelings and "bad" feelings--sort of like "good" weather and "bad" weather. We grow up believing the "successful" adult always has good feelings and is always happy. The person who fails at adulthood has bad feelings and, worst of all, can't control them.

We have come to understand this conditioning as the origin of self-hate.

Being taught my feelings are bad is the same as being taught I am bad.

We are trained from early childhood
to hide unacceptable feelings, which
results in depressing all our feelings.
It is possible to keep a lid on our
feelings, but not selectively. Keep one
kind of feeling hidden, and soon they
all must be kept hidden.

As a result, many
of us reach
adulthood having
learned to
depress our

feelings and now struggle with the
guilt and shame and hopelessness of
depression.

It is not possible

to depress our feelings

and not be

depressed.

"Losing It"

Sometime in the early 1960s the word began to get out that hitting a child as a means of discipline was not only abusive but ineffective as a method of educating the child in "proper" behavior. What hitting taught children most effectively was it is okay to hit other people.

Behavior specialists then began to promote the idea of "TIME-OUT." When discipline is called for, send the child to his or her room alone, set a timer, and allow the child back into relationship with you either when the timer goes off or when the behavior "improves" (that is, when whatever was driving you crazy has stopped).

I can't take it anymore!

When a parent sends a child into TIME-OUT, often it is because the parent feels stretched to the limit by the child's behavior, feels, in fact, as though she or he is about to "lose it," because it seems the child is "out of control."

But what does it mean to lose it? Lose what?

Take a moment to recall how you felt
the last time you thought you were
about to lose it. What was going on
inside you? How did your body feel?
What were you saying to yourself?

The parent feels out of control,
needs a break, and sends the child
away. When the child is gone, the adult
FEELS more in control. It SEEMS to
be working.

WHEW!

The idea of losing control assumes that we are in control. This assumption is where the breakdown occurs. Parents lose it because they believe they are supposed to be in control.

But control is an illusion. There is no such thing as control, only the appearance of control which is maintained by pushing our feelings down, by depressing our emotions.

The real loss happens long before we feel we are about to lose it.

The real loss
is not having the full experience
of our feelings.

When an adult is about to lose it,
what is really happening is feelings
that are always there and depressed
are threatening
          to break through and be seen,
                    to be consciously felt.

We are conditioned to BE HAPPY. If we are happy, we believe we are being the "right person." This means we are "good."

If we are sad, mad, confused, or afraid, we believe we are being the "wrong person." This means we are "bad."

So we learn to be even-tempered. We never want to be "out of control," which is seen as being "childish."

The belief is that to have emotions take over makes us bad, so we become masters at rationalizing ourselves out of our feelings.

Therefore, a "good" parent
teaches the child

ALWAYS "KEEP IT TOGETHER."

And when,
inevitably,
a parent loses it,
explodes,
and feels guilty,
the conclusion is

"I am a bad parent."

It never occurred to me to look inward, to myself, to see what needs of mine were not being met. I did not realize how tired and drained I was-- that I actually had nothing left for Alix. I took her behavior as a personal attack, and the interaction between us degenerated into a power struggle.

★★★

Go inside yourself for a moment and notice your breathing. Are you aware that you are breathing? Is your breath slow, fast, even, ragged, shallow, deep?

What are you feeling right at this moment? How do you know what you are feeling? Where did you look to find the answer to that question?

That feeling of about-to-lose-it is a gift. It is a signal that a need is being neglected.

It is sort of like emotional hunger pangs. When you get really hungry, you do not consider that you have lost it. You might have learned that it is not helpful to get that hungry because when you do you tend to gobble your food, eat the wrong things, overeat...

It's not a good system.

But does letting yourself get that hungry make you a bad person? No, of course not. It makes you a person who is out of touch with your body.

When you get to the point of screaming with anger or frustration, does that make you a bad person? No. It makes you a person who is out of touch with your feelings.

Screaming, then, is to emotions as gobbling is to hunger.

When we've gone too long without a basic need being met, our reactions become

HUGE.

There you are screaming, and you say,

"Well, I'm certainly in touch with my feelings, NOW!"

Stop and ask yourself:

"What happened right before I started screaming?"

"Could I have noticed that sooner?"

"What signals was I getting that I was becoming upset?"

With practice you will be able to notice these signals earlier and earlier.

CYNTHIA AND RICKY

Cynthia told about the afternoon she slid the refrigerator into its new home in the kitchen only to discover that in the process she had torn a section of newly installed linoleum. She was upset but just continued arranging things in the kitchen--until her four year old son Ricky began pounding the pegs into his carpentry set. And pounding. And pounding.

Cynthia found herself screaming at him. "Stop that awful noise! You're giving me a headache!" She stopped to take a breath after she heard herself and realized almost immediately that screaming at Ricky was really screaming about the torn linoleum. Ricky was just playing carpenter, and most days she would have encouraged him with comments like, "Aren't you having fun!" But today she had depressed the feelings of sadness and anger and disappointment about the torn linoleum, and those feelings found the next available outlet in losing it over Ricky's pounding.

***

"Losing control" is really about finding feelings that have been neglected and now refuse to be ignored.

The crucial information is what happens inside ourselves right before we "lose it."

Take a few moments and allow your attention to rest gently on your breathing. If you notice places of tension in your body, simply let your breath embrace those places so that when you breathe out you feel the tension dissolving. Quietly ask, "What feeling have I been ignoring or avoiding?"

It's okay to lose it.
It's one way to get in touch
with your feelings.

No need for guilt.
Parenting can be difficult.

Be gentle with yourself
as you would be with your child
or another loved one.

Of course, it's natural to avoid our feelings if we find them uncomfortable. It takes practice to get in touch with them and more practice to accept them as they are.

One step at a time,
that's all that is needed,

and you are doing it.

"The Story"

Acknowledge it, accept it, let it go.

We have been focusing on emotion, probably the single most difficult aspect of parenting. Another aspect we can bring consciousness to is

"The Story."

The Story is the running commentary in our heads. It's everything we tell ourselves about what something means and what will happen. It is usually a fear-based story that creates stress and anxiety about parenting.

The Story is based on beliefs, assumptions, standards, judgments, ideals, worries, prejudices, and other such notions we were taught as children and have never thought to question. We bring this baggage, this conditioning, to parenting and wonder why we struggle.

If I take time for myself people will think I'm selfish and immature. My child will feel neglected. I'll feel too guilty!

NO!

Until we are willing to STOP and tune in to The (Never-Ending) Story our conditioning controls us with, we believe what it tells us. But when we step back and observe instead of believing The Story, its grip on our lives loosens.

Learning not to believe
"The Story"
is a crucial part of
modeling successful adulthood
for children.

For instance, one of your children is sick and is staying home from school.

"The Story" is all the thoughts, all the "stuff," conditioning is telling you about what this means, how this is going to affect the day, how the things on your list won't get done, how you won't have time alone now...whatever the comments are for you; that's The Story. What is actually happening is that your child is sick. Period. The Story has nothing to do with what is actually happening, but has everything to do with making you feel...What? Overwhelmed? Despairing? Scared? Frustrated? Guilty? _____?

The Story is an unnecessary accessory after the fact. "I'm tired. Oh gosh, what if my daughter needs me to get up in the middle of the night again. I won't get enough sleep, and I'll be even more tired tomorrow. It's going to be an awful week...." The fact is I feel tired. The Story is everything that follows.

HOW to teach children what we really hope they will learn is astonishingly simple:

We must learn to BE--to live--the way we want them to be. We must begin to find out who WE really are beneath the social conditioning we have lived with all of our lives.

How Do You Want Your Child to Be as an Adult?

Do you want your child to be repressed, to feel anxious and fearful? If that is the adult you want to produce, then be that way with your child.

If you want a child who has the full range of his or her emotions, then you must begin to allow yourself the full range of your emotions.

Once you are able to do that, once you know emotions are to be welcomed not rejected, your child will learn to do the same.

You must take care
of the child inside
your adult self
before you will be able
to take care of the child
you are raising.

Of course, we don't have the luxury of putting on hold parenting our external children while we learn to parent our internal children. We must parent both simultaneously.

This is another opportunity to model how you want your child to be as an adult: taking care of yourself as you take care of others.

Attuning

Consider the infant with its very basic needs. When we hear it cry, we listen for a moment to hear the need being expressed.

Is the baby hungry? tired? wet? in pain? in need of company?

We attune as keenly as we can to determine what the need is, and then respond with food, a fresh diaper, some cuddle time--with whatever seems most likely to bring comfort to the child.

What if we were as keenly attuned to, and as motivated to respond to, OUR OWN NEEDS?

What if we notice a need (hear the cry), attune keenly to what is being expressed (anger, overwhelm, hurt, sadness, fear?) and respond to the need as appropriate?

Often all that is needed is for the need to be acknowledged and accepted, to be given undivided attention, to be allowed to exist. So we might say to the unhappy part of ourselves, "Oh, you're sad. Well, what would help right now?" or "What are you sad about?"

Ask yourself:
What am I experiencing in this
moment? What am I seeing? Hearing?
What sensations are happening in my
body? Where are they happening?
What emotions am I experiencing? Can
I accept how I am feeling? What do I
need right now? Notice whatever
comes up and try seeing each
moment of attention as a junction
with two possible paths:
- one leading toward the same old
suffering
-one leading toward acceptance and
freedom.

We would like to suggest that
unacknowledged feelings are crying out
just as an infant might
--and expressing the same need:
   to be recognized and responded to,
   to be heard and accepted.

"Yes but,
how can I learn to notice, respond to,
and accept my feelings? This sounds
so foreign to my way of being in the
world."

Most of us react to life out of the conditioning we received as children, much of which turned us away from ourselves and focused our attention outward.

That's okay, it's just helpful information to have because, in becoming conscious, we learn to turn our attention back inward and to find compassion for ourselves and our feelings.

Here are some steps we have found helpful ⇨ ⇨ ⇨ ⇨ ⇨

1.

Be present to your inner self.
Develop the same receptive
awareness for your own needs and
feelings that you have for your child's
needs and feelings. When you turn
your attention inward, stay present
and attentive long enough to
recognize and acknowledge whatever is
there.

Accept that you have needs. One of the most neglected, though essential, human needs is for attention (hard to accept after years of, "You're just trying to get attention!"). It is perfectly all right to want attention just because you want it.

Attune to what is needed. Just as over time you developed the capacity to tell the difference between your baby's cries of pain, hunger, and discomfort, allow yourself to hear and feel differences among your internal experiences.

4.

To the best of your ability, meet the need. This is often as simple (and as hard) as accepting what you feel without judgment, without trying to change anything, without hating yourself for how you are feeling. Perhaps just saying, "It's okay, it's okay."

Practice the four steps whenever
there is a moment:

When you first wake up
In the shower
As you take a walk
As you drive to work
In line at the bank
During a TV commercial

_____

_____

We have all had the experience of being with a child who falls down and skins his knee when Mom is out of earshot. He will cry for a moment or two and then seem okay again--until Mom comes into sight.

Then the tears start up, as agonized as ever. Mom comforts the child, and all is well once more. The little boy seems to need Mom to notice, attend to, and respond gently to the skinned knee, then life can go on.

WE need the same thing.

TIME-OUT

Plan a few minutes each day as your exclusive TIME-OUT. Treat this time as a gift to yourself, rather than as another "should" to burden your life. It's important to have quiet, alone time to create the inner peace our selves long to experience. Daily life, particularly for parents, is so filled with demands, distractions, and urgent must-do activities the opportunity for this kind of TIME-OUT gets lost in the shuffle.

Taking a daily TIME-OUT
might be the most important thing
you ever do.

When we take TIME-OUT for ourselves, even for only a few minutes, the struggling parts inside us know that someone cares, someone is paying attention to this struggling person.

Beginning to notice, acknowledge, and accept our inner feeling worlds requires practicing away from the normal non-stop busy-ness of everyday life. By practicing these four steps in a quiet place, you will become more able to follow them when the kids are bouncing off the walls, dinner is late, and you're exhausted from a busy day at work.

Here are the four steps again:
1. Be present to your inner self.
2. Accept that you have needs.
3. Attune to what is needed.
4. To the best of your ability, meet the need.

Whenever your awareness settles on

your inner process, allow that awareness to expand to fully notice your experience in the moment--the sensations in your body, the thoughts in your head, and your emotional state. You don't need to try to change your experience. It's just helpful to become aware of what's going on.

We rarely want to be "fixed." We long to be understood and accepted.

Once the idea of giving yourself time out has settled just a bit into your consciousness, it will be easier in times of stress for that critical pause to happen, the pause that creates the space for you to fully experience yourself as well as your loved ones.

Then, the next time you find yourself yelling at your kids and going into the countdown to explosion--

"I told you..."
"I need for you to..."
"You need to listen to me..."
"I'm warning you..."
"If you don't stop it right now..."
"I'm not going to tell you again..."
"One...two..."

--you'll increase your chances of stopping and modeling for your children the ways you hope they will treat themselves and those they love.

Qualities We Want to Model

BEING:

fully self-expressed
engaged
present
understanding
kind
fun
accepting
supportive
attentive

_____

_____

_____

For a moment, turn your attention inward. What are you saying to yourself? How are you feeling? What is your breathing like? Your heart rate? Is there tension in your body? Do you want to scream? Cry? Throw things? What are your thoughts like? Are you scrambling for control? Are you trying to talk yourself out of what you are feeling? Can you accept whatever you are feeling and thinking? If not, how do you know it's not okay to feel what you are feeling and think what you are thinking? Where are you getting the information that it's not okay? Tune in and realize that's childhood programming. It's either the exact programming you received, or it is the opposite of the programming you received. Either way, it's internalization of standards you learned growing up.

> Those are the standards
> by which you judge yourself,
> your children,
> and all of life.

Acknowledging, accepting and letting go of childhood beliefs and standards, letting go of The Story, frees us to make more appropriate choices in the moment we're actually in.

As I began to look inside and ask myself what I was feeling, I saw these emotions:

-- anger at my burdens: job, single parenthood, my daughter's "bad" behavior
-- sadness and hurt that she would treat me this way
-- hate for the whole situation and resistance toward it
-- despair because this was not an acceptable way to be with my daughter.

On top of that, physically I was feeling tired and hungry.

***

"I Need a Vacation."

"Once I've seen what my feelings and needs are, how can I respond? What I really need is a vacation, and there is no time or money for it."

Check back with this voice that says, "I need a vacation." What would a vacation do for you? If we listen closely we can begin to hear what we need to provide for ourselves:

"I need a break from the voices in my head telling me everything that's wrong."

"I need a break from the tension in my body."

"I need a break from the pressure, the stress, the relentless demands of parenting."

How to Take a Mini-Vacation
Any Time You Want One

Parents need vacations much more often than they're ever going to have them -- like, perhaps, several times a day.

Here is a two-stage process for feeling like you're on vacation any time you choose.

The first stage is what we are talking about continuously in this book: developing the ability to turn our attention away from The Story in our minds, the endless self-talk that creates stress in our lives. Take TIME-OUT and come into the present moment: look at something beautiful, listen to a piece of music you love, sit in a garden for a few moments and feel the breeze and really be present to where you are and the life around you, rather than being caught up in The Story in your head.

The second stage is taking a break from our standards. You realize everything can't happen every day. Instead of doing ALL the laundry today, do one load, let the rest of it wait, and take a little time for yourself. Instead of preparing the completely well-rounded meal you idealize serving every evening, do something that is easier for you and perhaps more fun for your family.

Now perhaps a voice is saying something along the lines of, "But you never get the laundry done, you never fix a decent meal." That voice is the problem, not the solution. What your family needs even more than clean clothes and balanced meals is a parent who loves and appreciates him or herself, and who brings that love and appreciation to the rest of the family.

Start thinking in terms of finding little breaks, little vacation moments, during the day. Include your children if that would feel good. Start with one minute and work up to ten.

Develop a list of things that actually take care of you and that require only a few minutes to enjoy. Choose things to consciously bring into your life because they nurture you.

If you "come to" and find yourself on the couch eating junk food and vegging out in front of the television, one of the kindest things you can do for yourself is not beat yourself up for having done it (remember the part about lowering your standards?). In

95

fact, you could say to yourself, "Well, I really needed that, I needed a little time for myself. Now I will get back to making the list of things that would really take care of me."

TV and junk food can make us feel good for a while. . .until the beatings start. Then we get told how weak, disgusting, undisciplined and basically WRONG we are for indulging ourselves. When we are able to take a few minutes in the garden, listen to music, or pet the cat, we can move to a place not only of feeling good but of feeling good about ourselves, which seems to be something we all deeply want.

We can model for children being in the present and enjoying life, sharing our good feelings as well as our struggles. "Oooo, isn't kitty's fur soft?" "Hey, come here and smell this great flower."

We are conditioned to try to escape from life, and that's what leads us into the kinds of behaviors that really don't take care of us. It's fine to eat junk food. It's fine to watch TV. It's fine to drink a beer or have a glass of wine. But that's not what really takes care of us. How do we know that?

> It's not what we would
> wish for our children.

The following is an exercise we have found helpful in guiding us to the responses our deepest selves long to receive.

Imagine that you are with an infant, small child, puppy, or kitten. As images arise, choose the one that tugs hardest at your heart, the one you feel most deeply.

Now imagine that little creature is upset, sad, hurt, or lonely. What would you say to that little being? How would you comfort it?

Can you find ways to be with this helpless little one that allow it to feel fully accepted by you?

Take a little time to find ways of
responding that feel right for you.
Now, try saying these same things to
yourself, to your
own needy inner
self.

What is doing that exercise like for you? Take a few moments to write down your responses.

Here are phrases others have come up with to say when doing the preceding exercise:

"I love you."
"It's okay to feel what you're feeling."
"I know you're afraid. I won't leave you."
"I won't abandon you no matter what."
"I know you are doing your very best."
"I understand."

A vacation would be nice, and since it isn't possible, perhaps your inner self would like to hear:

"I know you'd like the kind of vacation where you get to go away somewhere, and it's really frustrating not to be able to take one."

It would like to hear that you understand and accept how it's feeling.

Is it time to give yourself
a break?

Are you ready for some

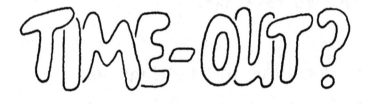

As children get older you can explain
your *TIME-OUT*. Why you want it, why
you do it, why you need it. You can
model it for them, so they will have it
for themselves in a world that calls
time for oneself "selfish."

Humor

One of the great kindnesses we can do for children is to bring some humor and levity into parenting. Many parenting difficulties originate with differences in mood. For example, I'm upset and irritable over something unrelated to my child. My child is also upset and unhappy about something and is whining or acting out in ways I find annoying, which adds to my irritability. This is a volatile situation. I'm trying not to react to the child in off-center, hurtful, harmful ways, trying not to take out my frustration on the child. But I'm in a pretty humorless place. It will be helpful to remember a couple of things:

1. What I'm going through with this child is perfectly normal. All parents go through it. There is no such thing as a perfect parent who is never stressed, never irritable or impatient or short with a child. It's normal.

2. We're both going to live through it. It's going to pass. If I can remember this, I have a chance to bring a little lightness to the situation.

When I remember this calmer perspective, I can initiate a discussion with my child and talk about some of the ways we both might "lighten up."

For instance:

Let's acknowledge that we are both
irritable, we're both having a hard
time, and
--let's see who can stamp their feet
the loudest.
--let's see who can jump the highest
and scream the loudest.
Now let's acknowledge that the
trouble we're having is not because
of what one or the other of us is or
is not doing. Let's remember that
the hard time we're having is
temporary, but our relationship is
permanent. Let's remember that we
want to be in relationship with one
another and remind ourselves of the
way we want our relationship to be.

We're not feeling particularly light-hearted, happy, loving, or kind. But we can remember to do something that is going to help us both get back to the kind, fun, loving, caring way we want to be with one another.

Pick Your Battles

I watched a grandmother trying to feed her 10 month old grand-daughter. The baby was in her highchair, eating one kind of food off of the tray and

being fed something else from a bowl. The child clearly preferred the food on the tray. I watched in fascination as the battle began. Grandmother was requiring this child to eat what she wanted her to eat, in the order she wanted her to eat it. When the child didn't want to, grandmother's control issues came to the fore. The baby's mother made some quiet conciliatory noises, but grandmother was having none of it. She actually said, "You know, if you let her get away with this at this age, by the time she's four she's going to be impossible."

As a parent, it's important to pick your battles. Ask yourself, "Does this feel important enough to get into that kind of power struggle with a small child?"

If you can STOP in the middle of an already happening power struggle, fine. If you can't, get through the best you can and then take time-out and come back to your breath. What were you bringing to this; what were you taught;

what are you afraid of; what were you believing; do you really believe that? Do you really believe the child is harmed if you don't make her eat what you want her to eat in the order you want her to eat it? (Substitute your particular content.) Could you let her make this small decision, knowing there might be a larger, more important situation in which you would like to exert your influence, and not have it be just one more power struggle?

Getting clear about motivations can be very helpful.

Are you doing what you're doing from a deep sense that this is important and valuable?

Are you doing it because it was done to you?

Are you doing it because you never examined this?

Are you doing it because you are already upset about another situation and you're bringing that upsetness to this one?

Take the time to stop and look, to

TIME-OUT CHAIR

pay attention, to be quiet, to be still with yourself. Bring the compassionate consciousness you want your child to develop to your own process, to what's going on with you, and, over time, clarity will come. Over time, you will find you are able to respond in a kinder more compassionate way in the moment, rather than simply reacting out of old, conditioned patterns of behavior from your childhood.

Suggestions for TIME-OUT Activities

--Imagine you are a balloon. Focus on your breathing, feeling the air as it enters your body and fills it completely. Feel the air as it leaves your body. Take ten breaths like this, just noticing what it's like to be a balloon.

--Label what you are feeling without using thought words. For instance, instead of "I feel angry," you might say, "I'm going to erupt like a volcano," or "I want to scream," or "A dinosaur is sitting on my chest."

--Let your feelings express themselves in images instead of abstracts. For example, if you are angry, rather than repeating The Story of the anger over and over in your head, imagine yelling out everything you would like to say to the person you are angry with, without censoring yourself. Focus your attention on your feelings instead of depressing them. Find a safe way to let energy out.

--Scream into a pillow or sit in the car with the windows up and scream.

--Pound a mattress with your fists.

--Dance using every part of your

body as energetically as possible, and pick music you really like.

--Run around the block as fast as you can. Again!

--Write about what you are feeling.

--Get out the crayons and draw a picture of your feelings

--How about some of your own ideas?

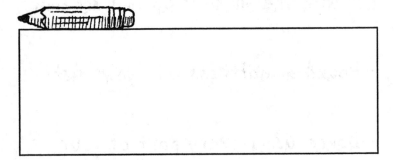

It's okay
to take *TIME-OUT* for yourself,
to take care of yourself.

In fact,
it's the best thing
you can do for yourself
and everyone you love.

Being with Your Child:
Modeling Self-Acceptance

When a parent is
    being true to him or herself,
a child knows it and can sense that
the parent is attuned inwardly.

This is the place we call CENTER.

Recall times when you are feeling calm and centered, and, from that place, imagine telling your child "no" in response to a request. Now remember times when you are not so centered, perhaps are grumpy and feeling over-burdened, and imagine telling your child "no" from that place.

How are those experiences different for you? Can you remember how you feel each time? How does your child respond to you in each situation?

Yes, it feels wonderful to be
centered and to act from that place.
But when we are stressed and off-
center in our feelings and actions,
 the best we can do
 is to accept that's where
 we are.

It's not easy being a parent. We
must be our own best friends,
accepting ourselves however we are.
 And it's from that place
 of acceptance and compassion
 that we can best model for our
 children.

Many adults believe it is upsetting to a child to experience an adult having an emotion like anger or sadness or fear. Yet how will a child ever learn to be okay with his or her feelings if all that is modeled is adults trying to pretend they aren't having feelings?

When we can be ourselves with our children, they will learn how to be with themselves because they will learn the self-acceptance we are modeling for them.

One way we can model the kind of
adulthood we wish our children to have
is as simple as talking, casually, about
what's going on with us.

Again, when we hide our feelings from
children, the only thing they learn is:
When I grow up, I'll have to hide my
feelings

because that's what grownups do.

When we can, instead, let them know what goes on inside us, without asking them to change or otherwise take care of us, we model being grown up.

Knowing about
an adult's internal processes
could be wonderfully beneficial,
especially as the child gets older.

Example:
I'm going along and I realize I'm feeling short-tempered. I stop (take a mini TIME- OUT) to check-in with myself: I say to the child, "Give me just a second. I realize I'm kind of short-tempered here, and I want to see if I can get a sense of what's going on with me." Maybe I realize

it's as simple as I had a cup of coffee this afternoon, haven't had anything to eat since, and my nerves are a little frayed.  So I say to the child: "Oh, I just realized I haven't had anything to eat, and I think I'm too hungry. Let's go get a snack. I just don't want to talk about anything until I've had a snack because I think that will make me feel better and solve most of my problems."

Another example:
As we're driving home I say to my child, "I had a really interesting day today. The boss came in and said

something to me, and I watched myself get really upset over it. But I thought about it for a minute and said, 'So are you saying that...?' and it turns out she wasn't saying that at all! I had misunderstood completely and got really upset over something that wasn't even true."

Most likely my child is semi-listening, semi-tuning me out but is taking in the information that it's okay to have problems, to face problems, to work though problems, to solve problems; that parents don't arrive just knowing everything and being perfect. This is going to save a lot of grief when this child is a teenager and realizes I, in fact, don't have all the answers and am nobody's idea of perfect.

We don't need to wait until we think a child is old enough to understand. We can talk to a child of any age, casually, about how life works. Giving them all sorts of information about the world they're coming into creates a relationship with us in which they feel comfortable communicating. Then, when they are older and upset or concerned, they will have language to express themselves and assurance of our support.

Revealing our inner process fosters an atmosphere of openness and trust. Keeping silent about our inner worlds, while asking a child to be open and vulnerable, can create distance and lack of trust.

As we become aware of our internal experience during difficult interactions, we usually realize that the same situations arise again and again.

THIS EXASPERATING REPETITION
IS A BIG HINT
THAT OUR HABITUAL RESPONSES
NOT ONLY DON'T WORK,
BUT NEVER HAVE.

This awareness frees us to try something new.

127

GEORGE AND SUZIE

George had a long day at work and then had to pick up his nine year old daughter, Suzie, at her after-school program. He was tense as she got in the car because he knew her habit of talking non-stop about her day as they drove home. She started to tell him what her friends had been talking about and he shouted, "I don't want to hear it. Just be quiet for once!"

Later, when he thought about it, George became aware that this was a scene that happened over and over, not just with Suzie but with his wife and others. When George was able to take time-out to be with himself and see what was going on inside, he saw that he wanted attention, he wanted to talk about a difficulty he was experiencing at work.

What George also realized was that he tended to be a non-talker, to not talk about his day fearing someone might say to him, "I don't want to hear about you."

When he picked Suzie up at school the next day, he listened to her for a while and then said, "You know, I'd love to tell you a little about my day. How about if you talk for five minutes, and I listen to you, then I talk for five minutes and you listen? You keep time, okay?"

★★★

As we watch closely enough to be able to interrupt old patterns with new responses, other, troublesome, repetitive interactions begin to shift, too.

New responses arise to replace tired, old ones, and the energy between parent and child changes

from the energy of conflict to the energy of mutual enjoyment.

The point at which a different choice
becomes possible is when we become
aware that we are about to launch
into an old

been-trying-it-forever-
even-though-it-never-has-worked-
behavior.

Just as you've begun to ask yourself,

"What do I need?"

you can ask out loud,
including your child in the question,

"What would help us right now?"

We listed several exercises on pages 114-116. Here are a few more:

See who can make the funniest noise.

See who can express their feelings in the funniest way

in the loudest way

in the softest way

in a dance

in a song

in a poem

Come up with some ideas that are just for you.

Allowing Children
to Be Themselves

Once you have found ways to be with your feelings in an accepting way, and once you have found ways of truly being yourself with your child, the next step is learning how to be with your child's feelings.

And the answer is quite simple: be with him or her in the same way you have learned to be with your own inner child--

1. Be present to your inner self.
2. Accept that you have needs.
3. Attune to what is needed.
4. To the best of your ability, meet the need.

Johnny is begging for that ice cream cone, and it's almost dinner time. You tell him, "No, this isn't a good time for ice cream." Can you just let him have his feelings-- disappointment, anger, sadness? "I know you're upset, Johnny. It's okay to be upset, but sometimes we can't have what we want."

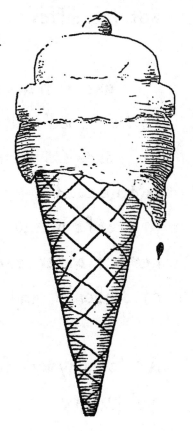

Notice.
Accept.
Respond caringly.

JAN AND ALIX <small>CONTINUED</small>

Once I could look at my own feelings, it was easy to see that Alix behaved as she did because her feelings were not too different from mine:

anger that she had been needing to be "good" all day,

sadness because she missed me and needed my attention,

safe in my presence to express herself after enduring the restraints of school all day.

As for physical feelings, she was tired and hungry.

★★★

Allowing a child to be herself or himself does not mean the child is given license to behave in whatever ways she or he wants. It is important for both the child and the parent to know that the parent is always boss; that there are acceptable and unacceptable behaviors; that there are family rules that everyone, parents and children, must abide by.

Two Very Different Things

Having feelings and acting on them
are two very different things, and it
is crucial to understand the
difference.

We often confuse feelings and actions:

I can't have angry feelings,
or I'll hurt someone.

I can't allow my sexual
feelings to be conscious, or I'll
become promiscuous.

I can't let myself feel sadness, or I'll
start to cry and never stop.

I can't be too happy, or I'll bother
the people around me.

In fact, to feel our feelings we do not have to do anything or involve anyone else at all. We live in fear of our feelings, however, believing that if we allow ourselves to experience them, we'll run amok. The belief is:

> when feelings are controlled,
> behavior is controlled.

Yet it is our experience that just the opposite is true:

> when feelings are controlled,
> eventually behavior runs amok.

For example:
When we depress anger, sooner or later we find ourselves screaming at someone.

When we are not afraid of feelings,
when they are allowed to exist, it
seems they flow through rather than
build up until there is a big emotional
explosion.

When we just let the energy of
emotion be there, noticing how it
registers in thoughts
and body, when we
remember that
feelings are normal
and good, when we
accept how we feel,

emotional energy seems to go on for
a while and then be finished.

If I learn to use that energy in a way that benefits me, I will soon see that the emotion isn't destructive at all.

One of my favorite things to do when life is getting to me is to turn on loud, fast music and clean the house, top to bottom. Before long I'm no longer upset, the energy is dissipated, I've had a good time with myself, and the house is clean.

What is your experience of a feeling? What happens when you allow a feeling to arise, be noticed, be felt, and not be acted upon? See if you are able to find the willingness to let a feeling just be a kind of energy and not something you have to act on in any particular way.

As with anything new, this work takes practice. We must learn to attune to our own needs, to hear and be with the child within us.

We no longer need to see ourselves as "losing it." Instead, we are learning to find and reclaim the parts of us that were taken away so many years ago when we were taught that what we feel is bad.

We are learning to accept ourselves.

If we want to reassure ourselves
that there is
nothing wrong with us,
all the way down to the depths of our
being,

all we need is to recall the
sweetness, defenselessness, and
innocence of the children we love. This
proves to us that

the essence of a being
is goodness.

JAN AND ALIX

Paying attention and accepting both my own feelings and my daughter's dissolved the tightness and resistance and allowed me to open to other possibilities.

--I finally acknowledged my feelings to myself and fully accepted them as being okay.
--I fully acknowledged my daughter's feelings by asking her how she was feeling and letting her know it was okay to feel the way she did.

We treated our trip home differently--

prepacking a nutritious snack and going to a park near Alix's school before starting the drive. A wonderful new routine! I was able to drop my previous belief that this was impossible because I don't have time, have to get home and cook, do laundry, make calls, help Alix, etc.

Because we had both let go of so much suffering, we were energized by the new experience and arrived home happy and relaxed.

How I am with myself has made the difference. For me, the world has become a much friendlier place.

hill...
TIME
OUT.

About the Authors

Cheri Huber has been a student and teacher of Zen for over thirty years. She is the author of seventeen books including there Is Nothing Wrong With You, The Depression Book, and When You're Falling, Dive. She founded A Center for the Practice of Zen Buddhist Meditation in Mountain View, California, and the Zen Monastery Practice Center in Murphys, California. She conducts retreats and workshops around the United States and abroad. She is working with Living Compassion to bring aid to vulnerable children in Africa and is heading a project to create an international peace center in Assisi, Italy.

Melinda Guyol is a licensed Marriage and Family Therapist, and a Senior Monk at the Zen Monastery Practice Center in Murphys, California. She found a natural convergence between Zen Buddhism and western psychology when she began practicing both awareness training and psychotherapy more than twenty-five years ago. In addition to her training as a monk, she is a facilitator of the "There Is Nothing Wrong With You" retreats at the Monastery and maintains a small private psychotherapy practice in Murphys.

For a current schedule of workshops and retreats,
contact us in one of the following ways:

Website: www.thezencenter.org

Email: information@thezencenter.org

Zen Monastery Practice Center
P.O. Box 1979
Murphys, CA 95247

Telephone: 209-728-0860

Fax: 209-728-0861

For a one-year subscription to the Center's quarterly
newsletter and calendar of events, *In Our Practice*, send a
check for $12.00 along with your name and address.

There Is Nothing Wrong With You
An Extraordinary Eight-Day Retreat
based on the book
There Is Nothing Wrong With You: Going Beyond Self-Hate
by Cheri Huber

Inside each of us is a "persistent voice of discontent." It is constantly critical of life, the world, and almost everything we say and do. As children, in order to survive, we learned to listen to this voice and believe what it says.

This retreat, held at the beautiful Zen Monastery Practice Center near Murphys, California, in the western foothills of the Sierra Nevada, is eight days of looking directly at how we have been rejecting and punishing ourselves and discovering how to let that go. Through a variety of exercises and periods of group processing, participants will gain a clearer perspective on how they live their lives and on how to find compassion for themselves and others.

This work is challenging, joyous, fulfilling, scary, courageous, demanding, freeing, loving, kind, and compassionate—compassionate toward yourself and everyone you will ever know.

For information on attending, contact:
Zen Monastery Practice Center
P.O. Box 1979
Murphys, CA 95247
Ph.: 209-728-0860
Fax: 209-728-0861
Email: information@thezencenter.org

BOOKS FROM CHERI HUBER

Published by Keep It Simple Books & Zen Meditation Center
All titles are available through your local bookstore.

Call 800-337-3040 to order with a credit card.

Mail orders use this form or a separate sheet of paper. Fax orders:
209-728-0861. Send e-mail orders to keepitsimple@thezencenter.org.
Request a complete catalog of products. Visit www.thezencenter.org.

___ There Is Nothing Wrong With You*	0-9710309-0-1	$12.00
___ There Is Nothing Wrong With You for TEENS	0-9636255-1-X	$12.00
___ How You Do Anything Is How You Do Everything: A Workbook	0-9636255-5-1	$10.00
___ The Depression Book*	0-9636255-6-X	$12.00
___ The Fear Book*	0-9636255-1-9	$10.00
___ Be the Person You Want to Find*	0-9636255-2-7	$12.00
___ The Key… Is Willingness*	0-9636255-4-3	$10.00
___ Nothing Happens Next	0-9636255-3-5	$8.00
___ Sex and Money: A Guided Journal	0-9636255-7-9	$12.00
___ Suffering Is Optional	0-9636255-8-6	$12.00
___ That Which You Are Seeking Is Causing You to Seek*	0-9614754-6-3	$10.00
___ Time-Out for Parents*	0-9614754-4-7	$12.00
___ The Monastery Cookbook	0-9614754-7-1	$16.00
___ When You're Falling, Dive	0-9710309-1-X	$12.00

Books and tapes are also sold in discounted sets.

Name _____

Address _____

City_____ State_____ Zip_____

Please send the books I have checked above.

I am enclosing $_____

Postage and handling** $_____

7.25% Sales tax (CA only) $_____

Total amount enclosed $_____

* Also available on audiotape.
**Add $3 shipping for the first book and $1 shipping for each additional book.
Send payment (US funds) or Visa, Mastercard, Discover or AMEX number to:
Keep It Simple, POBox 1979, Murphys, CA 95247
Orders out of U.S. send double postage. Overpayments will be refunded.